Skyhorse Publishing books may be purchased in bulk at special discounts for sales promotion, corporate gifts, fund-raising, or educational purposes. Special editions can also be created to specifications. For details, contact the Special Sales Department, Skyhorse Publishing, 307 West 36th Street, 11th Floor, New York, NY 10018 or info@skyhorsepublishing.com.

Skyhorse® and Skyhorse Publishing® are registered trademarks of Skyhorse Publishing, Inc.®, a Delaware corporation.

www.skyhorsepublishing.com

10 9 8 7 6 5 4 3 2 1

Library of Congress Cataloging-in-Publication Data is available on file.
ISBN: 978-1-61608-347-2

Printed in China

RAW
DESSERTS

Erica Palmcrantz Aziz and Irmela Lilja

RAW
DESSERTS

Mouthwatering Recipes for Cookies, Cakes, Pastries, Pies, and More

Anna Hult, Photographer

Skyhorse Publishing

Contents

Welcome to a World of Raw Desserts!

Since our first book, *Raw Food*, Irmela and I have given raw food-curious enthusiasts tips for exploring raw desserts and treats. That's how *Raw Desserts* was created. It's an entire book filled with recipes for cookies, pastries, snacks, ice cream, mouthwatering drinks, and many other treats. The recipes in *Raw Desserts* will introduce you to delicious taste experiences, which will also nourish your body and awaken your vitality.

Many years ago, before I knew about the concept of raw food, my body felt out of balance. I went to a homeopathic doctor, and he advised me to stay away from sugar, flour, eggs, and dairy. I knew there were good intentions behind what he said, but it was as if his words meant the end of life's pleasures for me. He told me that he ate papaya and passion fruit as candy, something I couldn't relate to at all.

After my visit, I felt as if sweets, cookies, and pastries were forbidden territory for me. As a result, I over-indulged every time I allowed myself to eat anything sweet. Now that I've experienced raw desserts and treats, I know I don't have to choose between good and healthy—I can have both at the same time! And I want to share that experience with you.

Today my lifestyle is high raw vegan, which means I eat primarily raw foods. I love all the good things life has to offer—and the fact that I can enjoy them. Sweets and desserts made the raw way are in my family's daily diet: cookies served with a glass of almond milk, rich chocolate mousse cakes, and refreshing ice cream!

When we make our raw goodies, we choose organic produce whenever we can; the taste is richer, has more nutrients, and is so much better for the environment. Whatever is left over after the food preparation can be used for composting, which will become fertile soil.

In this book, you also get to know Lillemor and Lisbeth, Annika and her family, and Jonas. We hope the interviews will inspire you to try different ways to prepare and make raw treats and desserts.

At the end of *Raw Desserts*, there is a picture of wild mint, which symbolizes our need for a balanced diet, using a lot of fresh vegetables and greens. The sweet and the good is what can make your day extra special.

Go raw—your way!

Erica

ERICA PALMCRANTZ AZIZ inspires people to change their life habits through lectures, courses, and events about raw foods. She lives in Gothenburg, Sweden, with her husband, Sam Aziz, and daughter, Saga. Erica discovered the benefits of raw foods while visiting her cousin, Jinjee Talifero, who lives with her husband and five kids in California. They eat only raw, organic, and local produce. And raw food has been a natural choice for Erica for the past five years.

About raw treats: "It feels luxurious to start the day with a berry pie and cashew cream. These are pretty much the same ingredients we would normally have for breakfast—berries, nuts, and fruits—but recreated in a new and delightful way!"

Favorites: "Some of my favorite everyday moments are when I'm enjoying a White Chocolate Truffle melting on my tongue, or indulging in Apple Cream and Vanilla Sauce on a sunny fall day, or when I need extra energy, a Hempseed Smoothie is perfectly silky and smooth."

IRMELA LILJA is a health and personal development journalist, and lives in Stockholm, Sweden, with her daughter, Ebele. Irmela eats mostly vegetarian food that she varies with raw food.

About raw treats: "A café visit usually begins and ends with a cup of tea for me. Those who see me probably think I'm so healthy and diet conscious. That's not even half true. I've always had a big sweet tooth, but I simply don't feel good after I eat regular cookies, cakes, and desserts.

"Nowadays I try to eat with this useful insight in mind: it should taste good in my mouth as well as feel good for my entire body. Otherwise, my enjoyment is short-lived. I cannot claim that I always succeed with this, but one thing's for sure: working on this book full of treats has been a dream for me! The preparation and tasting of Erica's recipes was always accompanied by my delighted exclamations!"

Favorites: "The Strawberry Cake, Pear with After-Eight Feeling, and the Sweet Dreams Cookies are all super delicious."

Read This Before You Begin!

• **Treats and desserts** are our mutual terms for all goodies in this book.

• **Though all recipes** specify number of portions, the numbers are approximate, depending on whether you plan to eat the treats as a snack or a dessert, what types of foods you ate before, and if you are serving to adults or children.

• **Fresh fruits and berries** need to be rinsed before you begin preparing the treats and desserts. How thorough you should be depends on if you bought imported fruit, or if you plucked berries from your own garden. Some people also prefer to rinse dried fruits and nuts thoroughly.

• **Dates** appear in many of the recipes because they are excellent sweeteners. If using fresh dates, take out the seeds before incorporating the fruit into the recipe. For best results, dried dates should soak for at least three hours prior to using. Medjool dates are called the kings of dates because of their size, taste, and juiciness. If you use these big dates, you can halve the amount the recipe calls for.

• **Cashews** add a delicious and smooth flavor to a dessert. They are an excellent replacement for cream or butter in "regular" treats and desserts, and therefore frequently appear in these recipes. Cashews have often been steamed to make them easier to peel. If you want raw cashews that have been opened by hand, you can buy them at health food stores, or order them online. When I don't have raw cashews at home, I go for the next best choice: organic and natural. You can exchange your cashews for other nuts or seeds; experiment and see what suits your taste buds.

• **Always choose** nuts and seeds that have not been roasted or salted!

• **Keep nuts** in the fridge if you have room. Otherwise they run the risk of going rancid, because they contain (healthy) fats.

• **When you put together a menu** of several raw goodies, choose wisely from the recipes so you get a nice variety. For example, a pie with a "nutty" bottom and a ball with a lot of nuts match well with a treat that contains primarily fresh fruits and berries.

• **Think about balancing** your meals when you serve dessert after dinner. After a light salad, it's appropriate to choose something rich, "nutty," and maybe chocolaty. After a steak, you might want to end the meal with lots of fruits and berries.

• **If you are vegan,** exchange the honey for agave nectar, soaked dried fruit, or maple syrup.

• **How long do the treats last?** The expiration dates vary widely: ice creams should be eaten right away, balls are good for about a week, and the dried crackers can last up to six months. Keep in mind that the recipes in *Raw Desserts* don't contain any preservatives, e-numbers, or trans fat (which is why a lot of store-bought sweets last a long time). The introduction to each chapter gives an approximate shelf life time for the treats and desserts

• **Choose organic** produce whenever possible. You will get more flavor and nutrients, and by doing so, you treat our planet with respect.

• **Raw treats are healthy?** Yes! But remember that the key to a healthy diet is balance, so incorporate a lot of fresh vegetables and leafy greens into your diet. Exchange your old snacks and sweets for raw treats, and feel the difference!

• **If you are allergic to nuts,** you can replace them with sunflower seeds, pumpkin seeds, sesame seeds, or coconut flakes.

• **In recipes** that call for a nut bottom, such as pies and pastries, you can adjust the bottom thickness, depending on how rich and "nutty" you want it to be.

Key Lime Raw Pie
Find it on page 26.

Raw Treats are Easy to Make!

Raw treats are not only delicious, they are incredibly easy to make. All you need to make piecrusts, cookies, and mousses is a food processor. A mixer is the best option for preparing raw whipped cream, smoothies, and other velvety goodies. You barely need an oven, except when you make cookies and crackers! Raw foods are cooked at 108°F or below to preserve natural nutrients that are destroyed when overheated. Some ovens make it possible to cook food at a very low temperature, but your best option is a dehydrator. It is easy to use, and enables you to dehydrate large quantities of treats. You can buy a dehydrator online, or at well stocked hardware stores.

The base for raw treats usually consists of nuts, seeds, and dried fruits and/or fresh or frozen berries and fruits. Take a look inside your pantry before you begin, and decide what you'll need to supplement what you already have. Many ingredients used in raw food cooking, such as nuts, dried fruits, organic vanilla powder, and agave nectar, have a long shelf life. Fresh fruit and berries can always be found in the grocery store, but if you keep your freezer stocked with frozen berries and bananas, you'll be able to mix together a delicious snack any time the sweet tooth kicks in!

Nuts and seeds are often soaked and sprouted before they are used in raw food recipes, so as to release enzyme inhibitors and make them easy to digest. The soaking process also removes toxins before consumption, and optimizes nutrition absorption. Some recipes call for soaking, while others recommend you use the nuts as they are. This is purely a taste choice, and the only reason why the recipe instructions vary; you always have the option to soak them. Sometimes it's recommended that you do the same to dried fruits, to soften them into a nice consistency so they mix smoothly with other ingredients.

Also, feel free to use these recipes as inspiration to create your own favorite treats!

This is Raw Dessert—raw food!

In *Raw Desserts* we treat you to delicious goodies and desserts made the raw way, with wonderful fresh fruits, berries, nuts, seeds, dried fruits, agave nectar, honey, and vegetable oils. All the recipes are natural, gluten free, lactose free, egg free, and free of processed sugars.

Raw food dishes are prepared with leafy vegetables, root vegetables, fruits, berries, nuts, seeds, sprouts, and seaweeds, as well as with honey and cold-pressed vegetable oils. The vitamins and minerals in these ingredients are preserved by being mixed together in their natural state, instead of being cooked together. Some are dehydrated, or water bathed in temperatures below 108°F.

Ingredients & Taste Adders

Most of the ingredients in these recipes can be found at grocery stores or well stocked health food stores. If some of them are new to you, you can read about them here.

Carob powder can be used as replacement for cacao. It has a chocolaty feeling, but with fewer calories. Carob also doesn't have the stimulating effect that cacao does, which I appreciate when I get chocolate cravings at night. It's made from the fruit from the carob tree, which grows primarily in the Mediterranean region. Most well stocked health food stores sell roasted carob powder if they don't have the raw kind, but you can always find raw carob online.

Goji berries are called the berries of youth in Chinese medicine. They are rich in vitamin C, iron, and beta-carotene. If you eat a handful (about one ounce) per day, you consume the recommended daily dose of antioxidants.

     The goji berry is also an excellent source of protein and essential fats. Use the berries as they are, or soak them for an hour or two. The soak water will turn orange like carrot juice, and you can use it for making smoothies and velvety creams. Remember to only buy organic goji berries! You can find them in well stocked grocery stores and health food stores, where you will also find dried cranberries, which are a good substitute for goji berries.

Hempseeds have a nutty flavor, and are great for making raw food milk. They are excellent in snacks or to roll treats in, and contain essential fats and complete protein. If you can't find hempseeds, you can use coconut flakes to make raw food milk and other snacks.

Cacao powder, bits, and beans: Raw cacao is made out of fermented cacao beans. You can peel and eat cacao beans as they are, add them to smoothies, or use them as a garnish. You can also add cacao pieces to ice cream and cookies, or sprinkle them on pies and cakes. Cacao is rich in magnesium, amino acids, antioxidants, and healthy fats, in addition to containing trace elements, and minerals. I always have a bag of cacao beans in my bag to beat my chocolate cravings!

     You can find raw cacao online or at health food stores, but you can also make the recipes with regular roasted cacao. Preferably, choose an organic and fair trade brand. You can also replace the cacao with carob in all the recipes.

Cacao butter is extracted through a process whereby cacao beans are cold-pressed. Cacao butter is firm when you buy it, and needs to be melted carefully in a water bath to achieve a liquid consistency. You can make lovely truffles out of cacao butter, but you can also use it as a body lotion.

Coconut oil: Did you know that the coconut is a seed, not a nut? Coconut oil always tastes better, and has a more distinct coconut flavor, when it is organic and cold-pressed. Keep it in your pantry. Always heat coconut oil carefully in a water bath; it will become liquid at about 86°F. Personally, I like to use it as a body lotion, as it softens my skin and smells delicious.

Maca powder comes from the South American maca root, which is said to increase performance, recovery, and libido. It contains complete protein, and high levels of iron and calcium. I often add maca powder to snacks and smoothies. You can find it online, and at well stocked health food stores.

Spirulina is a green sea algae powder that contains all essential amino acids, and is rich in minerals, such as calcium, zinc, and magnesium. Spirulina adds a cool color to your drinks and creams. I often add it to my daughter's Cashew Cream—it makes it more fun to eat, and even healthier!

Vanilla powder comes from organic vanilla pods that are ground into a fine black powder; it smells fantastic, and tastes delicious. You can find it in well stocked health food stores and grocery stores.

Natural Sweeteners

When we make raw treats, we use honey, agave nectar, or fresh dates. If you are strictly vegan, you can exchange honey for agave nectar, maple syrup (although this is not raw), or soaked dates.

Agave nectar is extracted from the cactus flower, and there are many different brands on the market. Some are raw, while others are not, so always read the labels on the packaging. Agave nectar has a low glycemic index, which means it releases glucose slowly, instead of spiking up blood sugar levels, like many other sweeteners do. Imagine a blend of maple syrup and honey—that's how agave nectar tastes!

Honey: If it's organic and locally produced, it's usually raw. Most of the time, it's specified on the packaging label, but if you want to be certain, you can contact the bee farmer.

Dates: Take out the pits, and use the fresh dates as is. Dried dates are easier to handle if you soak them first; they will soften and become easier to blend with other ingredients. There are many different kinds, but Medjool dates are called the king of dates because of their size, sweetness, and wonderful flavor.

Spicy & Yummy

You can enhance the flavor of your raw treats and desserts by adding spices, herbs, and eatable essential oils. Herbs are beautiful to keep in your kitchen window, and practical when you need to add something fresh and tasty to your food. Essential oils are very concentrated; start with just a few drops. Here are some of my favorite spices, many of which are incorporated into the recipes. Use the list below as inspiration to create your own variations of the goodies!

Spices: cinnamon, cloves, cardamom, dried ginger, dried chili, cayenne

Essential oils: peppermint, ginger, lavender, orange, lemon

Herbs: mint, lemon balm, cinnamon basil, basil

Miscellaneous: vanilla, goji berries, lemon peel, orange peel, lime peel, licorice powder, carob powder, and cacao powder

Pies
—DELICIOUS TO ENJOY EVERY DAY

When I hear somebody mention "pie," I feel happy in my mouth, body, and mind. You can vary these recipes, depending on what ingredients you have at home, and what you're in the mood for!

Berry Pie à la Dahls
4 portions

It looks like a traditional berry pie, but contains no flour, butter, or refined sugar. And it doesn't even sit in the oven!

BOTTOM:
2 cups walnuts
heaping 1/2 cup coconut, shredded
1 tbsp. honey
8 dates, fresh
2 tsp. cinnamon
pinch of salt

FILLING:
2 cups raspberries and blueberries, fresh or defrosted

SERVE WITH:
Cashew Cream, page 121.

1. Chop walnuts finely in a food processor.
2. Add coconut, and mix again.
3. Add honey, dates, cinnamon, and salt. Run food processor again.
4. Press dough into a pie dish.
5. Put raspberries and blueberries on the pie bottom.
6. Serve with Cashew Cream.

Pineapple Pie from Sälen
4–6 portionS

Mountains, fresh air, skiing—and far away from the store! Let your creativity abound on your ski vacation, and come up with something delicious out of the ingredients you find in your cabin.

BOTTOM:
3 cups almonds
10 dates
3 tbsp. honey
pinch of salt

FILLING:
scant 2 cups cashews
scant cup water
1/2 avocado
2 tbsp. honey
2 tsp. organic vanilla powder
1/2 big pineapple, cut into smaller pieces

1. Put almonds in a food processor, and mix until they turn into almond flour.
2. Add dates, honey, and salt. Mix again.
3. Press dough into a pie dish.
4. Mix cashews into flour in food processor.
5. Add water, avocado, and honey. Mix until you achieve a creamy consistency.
6. Mix again with vanilla powder. Transfer mix into a bowl and add pineapple pieces.
7. Spread filling over pie bottom.

Peppermint Pie

4–6 portions

The peppermint adds a nice freshness to this pie. Or you can choose to skip the bottom, and eat the filling as ice cream!

BOTTOM:
2 cups almonds
1/2 cup coconut, shredded
10 dates
pinch of salt

FILLING:
6 bananas, frozen
scant 1/2 cup coconut, shredded
3 tsp. organic vanilla powder
4–5 drops peppermint oil

1. Defrost bananas approximately 15 minutes.
2. Mix almonds in a food processor until they turn into almond flour.
3. Add coconut, dates, and salt, and mix again.
4. Press dough into pie dish.
5. Mix all ingredients for filling in food processor until creamy.
6. Spread filling over the bottom.
7. Serve pie immediately if you want to preserve the ice cream feel.

Key Lime Raw Pie

4–6 portions

I love to remake traditional recipes the raw way! Here is my variation of the key lime pie that one can find in Key West, Florida.

BOTTOM:
1 1/3 cups pecans
1/2 tsp. organic vanilla powder
2 tbsp. honey

FILLING:
scant 4 cups cashews
1 cup lime juice
zest from two limes
2/3 cup water
6 tbsp. coconut oil
4 1/2 tbsp. honey
1 lime, thinly sliced

1. Mix pecans in a food processor until they turn into pecan flour.
2. Add vanilla powder and honey, and mix again.
3. Flatten dough in a pie dish; you can use one with a removable bottom. The pie bottom should be crumbly and thin.
4. Mix cashews in food processor, until they become a floury mix.
5. Add lime juice and lime zest. Mix, and add a little bit of water until consistency is creamy.
6. Add coconut oil and honey. Mix again.
7. Spread filling over the bottom and garnish with lime slices.
8. Chill pie in the fridge for 2 hours before serving.

Succulent Strawberry Pie

6 portions

Coconut, lime, strawberries, and yellow kiwis—together they tickle your taste buds!

BOTTOM:
2 1/2 cups Brazil nuts
1 1/3 cups coconut, shredded
juice of 2 limes
7 apricots
1 tbsp. agave nectar or honey
scant 1/4 cup kiwis, sliced

TOPPING:
2 cups sliced strawberries
4 yellow kiwis, sliced

1. Soak Brazil nuts and apricots in separate bowls for 8–24 hours.
2. Mix coconut and Brazil nuts in a food processor.
3. Add lime juice, the water from the soaked apricots, the apricots, and honey or agave nectar, and mix everything in food processor.
4. Press mix into a pie dish.
5. Fill with strawberries and kiwis.

"Finally, desserts and sweets that I like!"

Adults and children in the Lundberg family like to spend time in nature, and Annika tells us she serves many outdoor meals and snacks.

"During boating season, we often have a picnic on a beautiful island, and when we walk or ski in the mountains, we bring a snack in the backpack."

The dining table at her home usually includes an eclectic mix of vegetarian dishes, fish, and sometimes even chicken. Annika's husband, Jonas, eats meat when he's invited to dinner at someone else's house. Nowadays, about 75 percent of Annika's summer diet consists of raw foods—"breakfast, lunch, a snack, and sometimes dinner"—and in the winter she incorporates into her diet about 50 percent raw foods.

"I like to eat warm vegetable dishes when it gets cold outside. I never think, 'Now I want to be a raw foodie.' Instead, I allow my instincts to guide what my body needs," she says.

Annika grew up in a family that was always interested in food and health. She, her mother, and her two brothers inspire each other to try new dishes.

"My brothers have been eating a lot of raw foods for many years. I have done it as well, but without being aware of the concept. I've been eating a raw food breakfast for several years, consisting of fruit, berries, dried fruit, seeds, and nuts. Sometimes I also eat oats that have been soaked in water. Today, the children and I have similar snacks throughout the day."

While many people fight their sugar cravings, it has been the exact opposite for Annika. She's never liked regular cakes, ice cream, and other sweets—not even as a child. For her birthdays, she used to get a papaya with cake candles instead of cake, but she views it as a positive thing that she didn't eat sweets.

Annika Lundberg, 41, lives in Billdal, Sweden, with her husband, Jonas, 48, and their children, Wilma, 10, and Jakob, 7. Annika manages her own yoga studio, Balance Yoga, and Jonas is a plastic surgeon. The entire family enjoys spending time outside, surrounded by nature, whether walking, skiing, boating, or golfing.

The best thing about raw treats: "They taste good! I've never been as delighted as I am now about cakes, cookies, and candy. I've finally found something I like."

The family's favorites: "Jonas likes brownies, Jakob likes the balls, Wilma really enjoys pies and chocolate mousse, and I like apple pie, carrot cake, and my own variation of the balls."

"I was very satisfied eating fruit and receiving a little bit of pocket money, instead of eating candy; I saved a lot of cash that way! Out of four siblings, I was the one who always had the most money in our household."

On the other hand, Annika's sister, Sussie, was always big on candy, cookies, and desserts. She couldn't believe her ears when she heard Annika was going to be part of a book about sweets.

"Sussie thinks that she is the perfect candidate for a dessert book, while I should be interviewed for a salad book," Annika laughs.

However, as soon as Annika tried sweets made the raw food way, she was hooked.

"I finally found something I like!"

Annika tried her very first raw food dessert at one of Erica's inspiration evenings.

"We got to try chocolate mousse and apple cake with pear-cashew cream. Oh, it was so delicious! It tasted fresh, without having a greasy and sugary aftertaste. I've never felt good from eating cream, butter, and other fats. I do eat a lot of nuts, though, and handle them well."

Annika's daughter Wilma, who joined her that evening, helped make the desserts.

"Right away, Wilma said, 'We can make this at home, too!' So now we make ice cream, mousse, and pies sometimes. We also make carrot cake."

Their son, Jakob, is very shy about trying new things, and he doesn't like fruit. He really enjoys the balls made out of nuts and dried fruit, though, and Annika makes a new batch every week.

"He wants to bring the balls with him to school, but that isn't possible, out of consideration to kids with nut allergies. On the other hand, the balls are great to eat whenever Jakob and I start to feel tired. He and I are the ones in the family whose blood sugar drops easily, especially when we're out skiing."

Since she started eating raw foods, Annika has experienced a notable difference in her "painful and often-occurring dropping blood sugar levels." She usually eats breakfast at 7, and before she discovered the raw way, she used to fill up on sandwiches once or several times to keep her satisfied until lunch.

"Now I often last the entire morning without extra eating. I also think yoga has created positive changes for me as well, and that my body has become more competent at absorbing nutrients and energy from food. When I do yoga, there's a huge difference in how I feel depending on what I ate the day before. I have more stamina and drive when I eat raw foods, and much less of a heavy feeling."

Loads of Ice Cream!

Frozen bananas serve as the base for raw food ice cream. Peel and cut them into pieces before freezing. Vary with different berries, fruits, and other taste enhancers. Choose organic citrus fruits when you add zest to the ice cream! Enjoy the ice cream right away, while it is creamy and cold.

Raspberry Ice Cream
2 portions

Raspberries make the ice cream perfectly pink.

2 bananas, frozen
heaping 3/4 cup raspberries, frozen or fresh

1. Defrost bananas and raspberries for about 10 minutes.
2. Put bananas and raspberries in a food processor, and mix until you get a creamy consistency.
3. Serve in two ice cream dishes.

Chocolate Ice Cream with Goji Berries
2 portions

You can round off the intensity of the cacao by sweetening the ice cream with honey, dates, or agave nectar.

3 bananas, frozen
1 tbsp. cacao powder
1 tbsp. honey, 3 dates, or 1 tbsp. agave nectar
2 tbsp. goji berries

1. Defrost bananas for about 10 minutes.
2. Mix bananas in a food processor until they are creamy.
3. Add cacao powder and any of the sweeteners. Mix again.
4. Put in a bowl and sprinkle with goji berries.

Banana Ice Cream with Lemon & Lime Zest
2 portions

The citrus peel adds tang and freshness. For more sweetness, drizzle agave nectar on top before serving.

2 bananas, frozen
zest of 1 lime
zest of 1 lemon
1 tbsp. agave nectar, optional

1. Defrost bananas about 10 minutes.
2. Mix in a food processor until you achieve a creamy consistency.
3. Add citrus zests, and mix again.
4. Serve in two bowls. Drizzle with agave nectar if desired.

Sunday Morning Luxury
2 portions

So simple, so yummy! Make the dream of a luxurious Sunday morning breakfast come true with frozen bananas, a package of blueberries, and Cashew Cream.

ICE CREAM:
1 package frozen blueberries
3 bananas, frozen or fresh
1 tsp. organic vanilla powder

GARNISH:
scant 1/2 cup Cashew Cream, page 121

1. If you are using frozen bananas, defrost for 10 minutes.
2. Put all the ice cream ingredients in a food processor and mix until creamy.
3. Serve in bowls, and dabble scant 1/4 cup of Cashew Cream into each and stir.

Mango Ice Cream with Cashews
2 portions

Do you want your ice cream richer? Make it out of cashews!

1 banana, frozen
1 small mango, frozen and cut into pieces
juice of 1 orange
4 dates
scant 1/2 cup cashews

1. Defrost the banana and mango for about 10 minutes.
2. Mix cashews in a food processor until they resemble flour. Transfer to a bowl.
3. In a separate bowl, mix the banana, mango, and the orange juice until creamy.
4. Add the cashew flour and dates, and mix again until everything is blended.
5. Serve in two bowls.

Tip: If you want the ice cream to resemble sorbet, skip the cashews and dates. Just mix together the orange, mango, and banana until you achieve a creamy consistency.

Banana & Mandarin Sorbet
2 portions

When you mix bananas with freshly squee-zed juice, the consistency is not as creamy as in most raw food ice creams—instead it's frosty like sorbet.

2 bananas
scant 1/2 cup juice from a mandarin
*   or clementine*

1. Mix bananas and juice in a food processor.
2. Pour into ice cream dishes, or put in a freezer container with lid and store in freezer until frozen.
3. Take out the sorbet 10 minutes before serving.

Chocolate Cashew Ice Cream
2–3 portions

My very first taste experience of chocolate cashew ice cream was at a raw food restaurant in New York City. My longing for that taste inspired me to create this recipe!

1 3/4 cups cashews
4–5 tbsp. cacao powder
4 tbsp. honey, agave nectar, or 8 dates
scant cup water

1. Mix cashews with scant 1/2 cup of water.
2. Add cacao powder and honey, agave nectar, or dates, and the rest of the water.
   Mix again.
3. Pour into ice cream dishes, or a freezer container with lid, and put into freezer until ice cream is frozen.
4. Let ice cream defrost 10–20 minutes before serving.

Soft and Smooth with Blackberries
2 portions

My daughter Saga absolutely loves avocado ice cream! It's a perfect snack for children with ice cream cravings.

1 avocado
8 ounces blackberries, frozen
1/2 tsp. organic vanilla powder
5 dates
a few twigs of basil or lemon balm

1. Let blackberries defrost for 10 minutes.
2. Mix avocado and blackberries in a food processor until you achieve a smooth and soft consistency.
3. Add vanilla powder and dates, and mix again.
4. Serve in two bowls. Garnish with basil or lemon balm.

Creams
EVERYDAY YUMMIES FOR EVERYONE

Treat yourself and your family to authentic creams made out of natural fruits and berries. Forget about additives and dyes! These velvety goodies are the cream of the crop as a snack or a weekday dessert. Serve with nut milk, Cashew Cream, or raw Vanilla Sauce.

If you add less water to the cream recipes, you will get jam instead.

Add a little bit of fresh lemon juice, which is a natural preservative, and the jam will last for a week. Store in the fridge in a tightly sealed jar. Vary the flavors by trying out our suggestions on pages 16–18.

Almond Milk
4 portions

Almond milk is easy to make. You can soak the almonds overnight to "wake up" the almond and optimize nutrition. You can easily peel a soaked almond by swiping it between your index finger and thumb. Milk made out of peeled almonds is whiter in color, and tastes even better. The peeling takes a little bit of time, but I see it as a form of meditation—with gratitude to all the fantastic food we get to eat.

scant cup almonds, soaked overnight if desired
2 cups water
honey, or 4 dates, optional
cinnamon, cloves, organic vanilla powder, optional

1. Mix almonds and water in a food processor.
2. Pour the almond milk into a bowl through a nut milk bag or cheesecloth. You can also use a fine mesh strainer, pressing out the milk with the backside of a spoon.
3. If you wish to sweeten and/or flavor the almond milk, add honey, dates, or spices. Mix again.

Tip: If you make almond milk out of soaked almonds, it lasts approximately 24 hours in the fridge. If you choose to use almonds that have not been soaked, the almond milk will last for about 3 days.

Strawberry Cream

2 portions

Strawberry cream with milk...lovely in the summer, but also enjoyable all year long!

8 ounces frozen and defrosted strawberries, or scant 2 cups fresh strawberries
5 apricots
1 1/2–3 1/2 tbsp. water, or the water from the soaked apricots
1 inch fresh ginger, grated

1. Soak apricots 4–10 hours.
2. Mix ingredients in a food processor until you achieve a smooth consistency.
3. If you use fresh berries instead of frozen ones, add a little bit more water into the mix.

Apple Cream

4 portions

Make this yummy cream during the fall when apples are ripe and delicious!
Try making bigger batches, and freezing single-portion sizes.

4 apples
heaping 3/4 cup raisins, soaked
scant 1/2 cup water, or water from the soaked raisins

1. Soak raisins 1–4 hours.
2. Mix ingredients in a food processor until you achieve a smooth consistency.
3. Serve the cream as is, or with Vanilla Sauce.

Vanilla Sauce

4 portions

This sauce is smooth like velvet, and for children is much more delicious than the prepackaged kinds.

1 1/3 cup cashews
1/2 avocado
1 tsp. organic vanilla powder
1 tbsp. honey
1 1/3 cup water

1. Mix cashews with water in a food processor.
2. Add avocado, and mix again.
3. Add vanilla powder, honey, and possibly more water before you mix again.

Blackberry Cream

2 portions

8 ounces blackberries, defrosted, or scant 2 cups fresh
5 figs
1 1/2–3 1/2 tbsp. water, or water from the soaked figs

1. Soak figs 4–10 hours.
2. Mix ingredients in a food processor until you have a smooth cream.
3. If you use fresh berries instead of frozen ones, add a little bit more water into the mix.

Nectarine Cream

2 portions

2 nectarines, cut into pieces
7 apricots
scant 1/4 cup water, or the soaking water from the apricots
1 tsp. rosehip peel flour, optional

1. Soak apricots 4–10 hours.
2. Use a blender to mix ingredients until you have a smooth cream.

Blueberry Cream

2 portions

8 ounces blueberries, defrosted, or scant 2 cups fresh
6 apricots
1 1/2–3 1/2 tbsp. water, or the soaking water from the apricots

1. Soak apricots 4–10 hours.
2. Mix ingredients in a blender until you achieve a smooth consistency.
3. If you use fresh berries instead of frozen ones, add a little bit more water into the mix.

Raspberry Cream

2 portions

8 ounces raspberries, defrosted, or scant 2 cups fresh
6 dates
1 1/2–3 1/2 tbsp .water

1. Mix ingredients in a blender until you achieve
   a smooth consistency.
2. If you use fresh berries instead of frozen ones, add
   a little bit more water into the mix.

Erica relaxing in the grass with her husband, Sam, and their daughter, Saga.

Pastries & Cakes
HEAVENLY GOOD

These cakes are popular with adults and children, and are excellent at festive occasions. A cake demands a bit of planning and preparation. Invite your children to help you, and have fun together making the cake.

The cakes can be stored in the fridge for approximately twenty-four hours. You can also store the pastries in the freezer for months, and they are easy to defrost when you have unexpected visitors.

Srawberry Cake
4–6 portions

CAKE BOTTOM:
3 cups almonds
5 tbsp. honey
3 tbsp. olive oil, or rapeseed oil
pinch of salt

FILLING:
3 bananas, mashed
2 cups fresh strawberries, sliced

TOPPING:
2 cups Cashew Cream, see page 121

GARNISH:
2 cups fresh strawberries, whole or sliced

1. Mix almonds in a food processor until they turn into fine almond flour.
2. Add honey, oil, and salt. Mix again.
3. Press half of the cake dough into a cake dish.
4. Put half of the mashed bananas and sliced strawberries on top.
5. Add another layer by using 1/2 of the remaining cake bottom dough. Add another layer of bananas and strawberries on top.
6. Add the last layer of the remaining cake bottom.
7. Cover entire cake with Cashew Cream.
8. Garnish with whole or sliced strawberries.

Chocolate Mousse Cake

6 portions

Whenever I make this cake, I end up with a little bit of chocolate on my cheeks and nose. This is a cake for adult children—and anyone who loves chocolate!

CAKE BOTTOM:
2 cups walnuts
5–6 tbsp. cacao powder
pinch of salt
2 tbsp. coconut oil
2 tbsp. honey
15 dates
scant 2/3 cup Cashew Cream (use the variation without pear and agave nectar), see page 121

AVOCADO-CHOCOLATE MOUSSE:
scant 1/2 cup fresh dates
scant 1/2 cup water
4 tbsp. honey
1 tsp. vanilla powder
2 avocados
scant 1/2 cup cacao powder

TOPPING:
Scant 1/4 cup Cashew Cream, see page 121

GARNISH:
Choose between raspberries, blackberries, red currants, fresh apricots, and strawberries

1. Chop walnuts finely in a food processor.
2. Add cacao powder and salt, and mix again.
3. Add the rest of the ingredients for the cake bottom, mix, and taste to determine if you want it to be more "chocolaty."
4. Place the cake bottom onto a beautiful plate. Make it about 1 inch tall.
5. Make the chocolate mousse: Blend dates, water, honey, and vanilla into a nice medley in a food processor.
6. Add avocado and cacao powder. Mix until you have a creamy consistency. Stop food processor occasionally to scrape down the sides before you continue mixing.
7. Spread chocolate mousse on top of the cake bottom.
8. Decorate cake with Cashew Cream.
9. Garnish with your choice of berries.

Cashews Meet Blueberries

Approximately 12 pastries

I got the inspiration for these wonderful pastry recipes from Kristfrid Warner. A huge thanks to her because she is always spreading around delicious flavors and positive vibrations!

BOTTOM:

scant 1 cup cashews
1 tbsp. honey
juice of 1 lime

FILING/BLUEBERRY MARMALADE:

8 ounces blueberries, defrosted, or scant 2 cups fresh
6 apricots
3 tbsp. water for soaking (if you choose fresh berries), optional

TOPPING/CHOCOLATE SAUCE:

scant 1 cup coconut oil
scant 2/3 cup cacao powder
scant 1/4 cup agave nectar

GARNISH:

fresh blueberries, or berries of your choice

1. Soak apricots 4–10 hours.
2. Mix cashews in a food processor until they turn into cashew flour.
3. Add honey and lime juice. Mix again.
4. Press dough into baking cups, approximately 1/4 inch thick.
5. Mix ingredients for the blueberry marmalade.
6. Spread blueberry marmalade over the bottoms.
7. Make the chocolate sauce. Begin by melting the coconut oil in a double boiler.
8. Stir in cacao powder and agave nectar.
9. Pour chocolate sauce over the filling until covered.
10. Store pastries in the fridge or freezer until the chocolate is firm. If you keep them in the freezer, defrost for approximately 20 minutes prior to serving.
11. Decorate with fresh blueberries, or any berries of your choice.

Hazelnuts Meet Raspberries

Approximately 12 pastries

BOTTOM:
scant 1 cup hazelnuts
pinch of organic vanilla powder
scant 1/4 cup water

FILLING/RASPBERRY MARMALADE:
8 ounces raspberries, defrosted, or scant 2 cups fresh
6 dates
water (if you are using fresh berries)

TOPPING/ CHOCOLATE SAUCE:
scant 1 cup coconut oil
scant 2/3 cup cacao powder
scant 1/4 cup agave nectar

GARNISH:
fresh raspberries, or berries of your choice

1. Mix hazelnuts in a food processor until you have hazelnut flour.
2. Add vanilla powder and water. Mix again.
3. Press the dough into baking cups, approximately 1/4 inch thick.
4. Mix ingredients for the raspberry marmalade.
5. Spread marmalade over the bottoms.
6. To make the chocolate sauce, start by heating the coconut oil in a double boiler.
7. Stir in cacao powder and agave nectar.
8. Pour chocolate sauce over the filling until it is covered.
9. Store pastries in the fridge or freezer until the chocolate is firm. If you keep them in the freezer, defrost for approximately 20 minutes prior to serving.
10. Decorate with fresh raspberries, or any berries of your choice.

Blackberries Meet Pecans

Approximately 12 pastries

BOTTOM:
scant 1 cup pecans
1 tbsp. honey
2 tsp. rapeseed oil
pinch of salt

FILLING/BLACKBERRY MARMALADE:
8 ounces blackberries, defrosted, or scant 2 cups fresh
5 figs
3 tbsp. water (if you are using fresh berries), optional

TOPPING/CHOCOLATE SAUCE:
scant 1 cup coconut oil
scant 2/3 cup cacao powder
scant 1/4 cup agave nectar

GARNISH:
fresh blackberries, or berries of your choice

1. Soak figs 4–10 hours.
2. Mix pecans in a food processor until you have pecan flour.
3. Add honey, rapeseed oil, and salt. Mix again.
4. Press dough into baking cups, approximately 1/4 inch thick.
5. Mix ingredients for the blackberry marmalade.
6. Spread marmalade over the bottoms.
7. Make the chocolate sauce. Begin by melting the coconut oil in a double boiler.
8. Stir in cacao powder and agave nectar.
9. Pour chocolate sauce over the filling until it is covered.
10. Store pastries in the fridge or freezer until the chocolate is firm. If you keep them in the freezer, defrost for approximately 20 minutes prior to serving.
11. Decorate with fresh blackberries, or any berries of your choice.

Tip: Argan oil is a delicious substitute for rapeseed oil.

Earth Cake

4 portions

White as snow, green as grass, brown as earth, and red as the sunset.
This cake's colors remind me of the colors of nature—thus, the name!

BOTTOM:
scant 2 cups cashews
2 1/2 cups coconut, shredded
4 tbsp. honey
2 tsp. water or lemon juice

LAYER 1/GREEN CASHEW CREAM:
scant 2 cups cashews, soaked
scant 2/3 cup water
4 dates
4 tbsp. coconut oil
1/2 pear
1 tsp. spirulina powder

LAYER 2/ORANGE CAROB MOUSSE:
3 avocados
juice of 3 oranges
1 1/3 cups dates
6 tbsp. carob powder

GARNISH:
scant 1 cup goji berries

1. For the bottom, mix cashews in a food processor until you have fine cashew flour.
2. Add coconut, and mix until blended with the cashews.
3. Add honey and lemon juice. Mix again.
4. Flatten the dough into a small, deep pie dish.
5. Mix cashews for the first layer with water until you have a creamy blend.
6. Add dates, coconut oil, and pear. Mix again.
7. Add spirulina powder, and possibly more water. Mix again.
8. Spread a layer of green cashew cream over the bottom.
9. Mix ingredients for the orange carob mousse in a food processor until it is smooth.
10. Spread the orange carob mousse over the cake. Store your Earth Cake in the fridge a few hours.
11. Just before serving, garnish with goji berries.

Balls & Squares
SNACKS WITH SUPERPOWERS!

These are fun snacks that come in different flavors and shapes. They're like candy, but the kind you can eat every day! Raw snacks last about a week if you store them in the fridge. Keep them in the freezer if you want them to last longer. Feel free to double the recipe so you have an extra stash on hand when you get cravings, or visitors.

Hidden Maca
Approximately 10 pieces

Super snacks with maca and cacao.

1 1/3 cups almonds
2 tbsp. coconut oil
3 tbsp. cacao powder
1 tbsp. maca powder
5 dates

1. Mix almonds in a food processor until you get fine almond flour.
2. Add coconut oil, and mix again.
3. Add cacao and maca powder, and mix again.
4. Add dates, and mix again.
5. Form into balls, or spread in a square dish and cut into smaller squares.

Licorice Balls

Approximately 10

Delicious snacks with real licorice!

scant 1 cup almonds, or walnuts
1–2 tbsp. carob powder
pinch of salt
1 tbsp. coconut oil
2 tbsp. honey
1 tbsp. olive oil
2–4 tsp. licorice powder, or 2 tbsp. licorice root flour

1. Mix almonds or walnuts in a food processor until you have fine flour.
2. Add additional ingredients and 2 tsp. of the licorice powder. Mix again.
3. Taste, and add more licorice powder if needed.
4. Roll into balls.

Licorice Fudge

Approximately 10 pieces

When I used to eat regular candy, I really enjoyed the black licorice fudge cubes. Here is an entirely raw variation that tastes even better, and makes your body happy!

1 1/3 cups pecans
4 tbsp. honey
3 tsp. licorice powder, or 1 tbsp. licorice root flour

1. Mix pecans in a food processor until you have fine flour.
2. Add honey and licorice powder. Mix again. Taste, and add more licorice powder if needed.
3. Form into cubes, and store in the fridge for an hour or longer before serving.

Tip: Licorice flour is ground licorice root, and can be bought in health food stores. Licorice powder is the juice from the licorice root that has been refined into a powder, and you can buy it online.

Truffles

Approximately 10 truffles

Try a raw chocolate truffle and taste authentic cacao flavor. Feel free to experiment with your own variations; check out our recommendations on how to add natural flavors on page 16–18!

scant 1/2 cup cacao butter
scant 1/4 cup coconut oil
6 tbsp. cacao powder
3 tbsp. agave nectar

1. Cut cacao butter into small pieces before you carefully melt them in a water bath.
2. Add coconut oil to the cacao butter, and stir until blended.
3. Add cacao powder and agave nectar. Stir again.
4. Pour into ice cube tray and store in the fridge. They take about 2 hours to become firm, or less if you put them in the freezer.

Truffles with Minty Nut Cream

Approximately 25 truffles

Follow the instructions for the recipe above and add the minty nut cream.

A batch of the chocolate truffle, see recipe above.

NUT CREAM:
scant 1 cup macadamia nuts
scant 2/3 cup water
1 1/2 tbsp. agave nectar
2 tbsp. cacao powder
5 drops peppermint oil

1. Mix macadamia nuts with water.
2. Add agave nectar, cacao powder, and peppermint oil. Mix until creamy.
3. Fill an ice cube tray halfway with the nut cream, then pour the truffle batter to the brim.
4. Store in the freezer until the truffle batter is frozen, about 5 hours.
5. For best taste, take out the truffles from the freezer five minutes before eating.

White Truffles
Approximately 10 truffles

scant 1/2 cup cacao butter
scant 1/4 cup coconut oil
2 tbsp. agave nectar
2 tsp. organic vanilla powder

1. Cut cacao butter into large pieces, and melt in a water bath.
2. Add coconut oil, and mix until blended.
3. Stir in agave nectar and vanilla powder.
4. Pour into ice cube tray and store in the fridge.
   The truffles take about 2 hours to become firm,
   or less if you put them in the freezer.

Raw Dessert—Pure Happiness

Approximately 15–20 pieces

I came up with this recipe the day before the publisher's deadline for the manuscript. Buzzing with euphoria over the taste, I called Irmela and said, "This recipe has to be in the book. Where can we squeeze it in?" Then I went to Anna's photo studio to capture an image of the delicious delight. This bonus recipe tastes like something out of a fairy tale.

Walnuts and hempseeds provide us with healthy fats that fuel our brain power; goji berries provide antioxidants that strengthen our immune system; and raw cacao powder contains a nutrient that can increase our sense of happiness. Raw Dessert!

1 cup cacao butter, cut into pieces
1 1/3 cups walnuts
scant 2/3 cup hempseeds, shelled
6 tbsp. goji berries
4 tbsp. cacao powder
pinch of salt
1 1/2 tbsp. agave nectar
2 tsp. organic vanilla powder

1. Melt cacao butter in a water bath.
2. Chop walnuts coarsely in a food processor, or with a knife.
3. Mix walnuts, hempseeds, goji berries, cacao powder, salt, and vanilla powder in a bowl.
4. Pour cacao butter over the mix. Add agave nectar, and stir until thoroughly blended.
5. Spread in a square dish about 1 1/4 inches deep. Let it firm up in the fridge, about 3 hours.
6. Cut into squares and enjoy!

Cinnamon Gals

Approximately 10 pieces

This recipe was inspired by the American raw food chef Matt Amsden, and his yummy ball recipe, "Cinnamon Girls."

scant 1 cup almonds
scant 1/4 cup raisins
3 tbsp. honey
1 tbsp. rapeseed oil
1 tsp. cinnamon
pinch of salt

1. Mix almonds in a food processor until they resemble flour.
2. Transfer to a bowl. Add additional ingredients, and mix with a spatula.
3. Roll into balls.

Minty Balls

Approximately 15 pieces

Peppermint oil gives the balls a refreshing flavor that is reminiscent of white mint chocolate. Yum!

 2 cups cashews
10–15 drops peppermint oil
scant 1/4 cup honey
1/2 tbsp. water

1. Mix cashews in a food processor until it resembles fine flour. Add peppermint oil, and mix again. Add honey and water, and mix.
2. Roll into balls.

Coconut Fudge

Approximately 10 pieces

Cubes made with coconut and a touch of carob. I often cozy up at night with these because the carob doesn't keep me up the same way cacao does.

1 1/3 cup walnuts, plus scant 1/2 cup finely chopped walnuts
2 tbsp. honey
1 tbsp. water
scant 1/2 cup shredded coconut
2 tbsp. coconut oil
2 tbsp. carob powder

1. Put whole walnuts in a food processor and mix until you have fine walnut flour.
2. Put walnut flour in a bowl, and stir in honey, water, coconut, coconut oil, and carob. Add finely chopped walnuts.
3. Flatten the dough in a dish about 1 inch deep, and store in the fridge for about 1 hour. Cut into squares before serving.

Power Event Balls
Approximately 15 balls

The basic recipe for these balls comes from our first book, *Raw Food*.
This is a variation, with extra power added!

1 1/4 cups walnuts
scant 1 cup raisins
1 tbsp. maca powder
pinch of sea salt
scant 1/4 cup carob or cacao powder
1 tbsp. Almond Milk (see page 44), or water
5 tbsp. hempseeds, shelled

1. Chop walnuts coarsely in a food processor.
2. Add raisins, and mix again.
3. Add maca powder, salt, carob or cacao powder, and Almond Milk.
   Mix until batter can easily be rolled into balls.
4. Roll the balls in the hempseeds.

Tip: Roll the balls in coconut instead of hempseeds.

Hempseed Covered Apricots
Approximately 5 pieces

Apricots are rich in iron. They're good for everyone, especially women and children!

10 apricots
5 apricots, dried
3 tbsp. hempseeds, shelled
water from the soaked apricots, optional

1. Soak 10 apricots in water for 8 hours.
2. Use a food processor to mix the soaked apricots with the dried apricots. If necessary,
   add some of the soak water in order to mix the apricots properly. You should be able
   to form batter into balls.
3. Roll apricot balls in hempseeds.

Cashew Christmas

Approximately 10 pieces

Christmassy balls that are excellent—even in July!

1 1/2 cups cashews
3 tsp. cinnamon
2 tsp. ground cardamom
1 tsp. organic vanilla powder
1 tsp. nutmeg, grated or ground
scant 1 cup raisins
2 tbsp. agave nectar or honey
Chocolate Sauce, optional, see page 120

1. Mix cashews in a food processor until they turn into a fine floury mix.
2. Add spices, and mix. Add raisins, and mix again.
3. Pour agave nectar or honey into batter, and mix until you can shape batter into balls.
4. For added delight, roll balls in Chocolate Sauce. Store them in the fridge until the chocolate solidifies.

Spicy Snacks

Approximately 10 pieces

These are extra delicious on a cold winter day! Cloves and nutmeg are sure to warm you up.

1 1/3 cups walnuts
1 tbsp. carob powder
1 tsp. cinnamon
1/2 tsp. nutmeg, grated or ground
1/2 tsp. cloves
3 tbsp. honey

1. Chop walnuts into small pieces in a food processor.
2. Add carob powder and spices, and mix thoroughly.
3. Add honey, and mix again.
4. The batter is ready when you can roll it into balls or make other fun shapes out of it.

"I always prefer raw desserts!"

Jonas Faremo enjoys eating well, but lives by himself and does not prioritize dessert when cooking for himself.

"I am always pleasantly surprised when I find raw desserts at a café, and order it 100 times out of 100! I wish more places offered raw desserts."

Jonas grew up on regular home cooked meals, but nowadays, 30 to 50 percent of his diet consists of raw foods. He likes the light feeling and extra energy he gets from eating raw.

"My body deserves the best. When I discovered the positive consequences of eating raw foods, it became a natural choice for me."

This past Christmas, Jonas treated his parents, siblings, and friends to balls made out of raw gingerbread batter.

"They thought it was delicious! The best part was when I told them that it was healthy, too! It's probably a good idea not to tell people about the health benefits before you let them try the raw treats, because automatically they associate it with something bland and boring," he says, laughing.

Jonas really likes raspberry and blueberry pie—he's eating it as we speak—but apple pie remains his favorite. It was the very first raw dessert he tried.

"I didn't expect it to taste just as delicious as traditional pie. The combination of the sweet and sour apples, with cinnamon and the rich nut bottom, is genius!"

Jonas Faremo, 30 years old, works in trademark strategy and communications. His interests include personal development, riding his motorcycle, and leading an active lifestyle. "My three musts are jogging, going to the gym, and doing yoga—I love it all!" Jonas also recently discovered triathalon training: biking, running, and canoeing. He enjoys reading fiction, and Paulo Coelho is one of his favorite authors.

The best part about raw treats: "Pleasures are necessary in life. Raw goodies are delicious, without giving you a sense of heaviness."

Favorite raw treat: Apple pie!

Cookies & Crackers
—TO SATISFY THE COOKIE MONSTER IN YOU!

It's a pleasure to serve these cookies freshly baked, with a glass of cold Almond Milk. They're likely to disappear very quickly! If you double the recipe, you can fill your oven with cookie sheets. Use your regular oven if it has the option to bake at 108°F, but open the oven door frequently to release condensation. If you have a dehydrator (see page 15) you'll have to test it to know how long to keep the cookies in there.

Store the cookies in a tightly sealed container. They last for at least three weeks, and up to several months, depending upon how thoroughly dehydrated they are.

Sweet Dreams
Approximately 25–30 cookies

2 cups cashews
5 tbsp. water from soaked dates, figs, or apricots, or 3 tbsp. honey
3 tsp. organic vanilla powder

1. Mix cashews in a food processor until you have cashew flour.
2. Add water and vanilla powder, and mix again.
3. Shape into cookies and place on a cookie sheet. Bake 8–12 hours at 108°F, and rotate the pans in the oven after 4–6 hours.

Tip: If you use honey, the cookies get chewy, and you have to bake them a little bit longer. If you use soak water to sweeten them, they won't take as long to dehydrate.

Small Cookies with Superpowers

Approximately 20 cookies

Super foods have a lot of nutrients per gram. Bake them into little cookies and get plenty of energy and extra power!

scant 1/2 cup buckwheat
scant 1/4 cup linseed and scant 1/2 cup water
scant 1/4 cup shredded coconut
1 1/3 cup almond paste (leftover from making Almond Milk, see page 44)
scant 1 cup goji berries
juice of 1/2 lemon
2 tbsp. maca powder

1. Soak buckwheat overnight, or about 8 hours.
2. Soak linseeds in scant 1/2 cup water 1/2–4 hours.
3. Soak goji berries 1/2–4 hours.
4. Drain goji berries from the water, and mix them in a food processor with all ingredients, except for the buckwheat.
5. Transfer batter to a bowl.
6. Pour off the water from the buckwheat, and rinse thoroughly. Add to batter.
7. Shape into cookies and place them on a parchment-lined baking sheet.
8. Bake 8–10 hours at 108°F.

Choc Chip Cookie
Approximately 25 cookies

Cookies with cacao nibs—yum!

2 cups cashews
5 tbsp. soak water from dates or 2 1/2 tbsp. honey
5 tbsp. cacao nibs, or crushed whole cacao beans

1. Soak dates for at least 1 hour if you want to use the soak water.
2. Mix cashews in a food processor until they turn into cashew flour.
3. Mix cashew flour with soak water or honey in food processor. Transfer to a bowl, and stir in cacao nibs.
4. Shape into cookies and place on a baking sheet. Bake 8–12 hours at 108°F, and rotate pans after 4–6 hours.

Tip: Honey makes the cookies a bit tougher than the soak water, and they'll take longer to bake. If you want to speed up the process, use soak water to sweeten the cookies.

Cardamom Biscuits
25 small biscuits

Every time I bake these, you can smell them throughout the entire house. It's pure happiness to eat these freshly baked biscuits with a glass of cold Almond Milk.

3 cups almond paste, leftover from making Almond Milk, see page 44
1 1/3 cup linseeds, plus scant 1 cup water
1 cup dates
2 tbsp. ground cardamom pods or 1 tbsp. cardamom powder
2–5 tbsp. soak water

1. Soak dates and linseeds in two separate bowls, 2–6 hours.
2. Mix almond leftovers, linseeds, and dates in a food processor. Dilute with the soak water from the dates, one tbsp. at a time, until you get a porridge-like batter.
3. Grind cardamom yourself in a mortar (peel off the cardamom pod first), or use ground cardamom, and add to the batter. Add more cardamom to taste, or soak water.
4. Using a little batter at a time, shape into biscuits. Feel free to use a glass to create a nice round shape. Fill two baking sheets, and put into oven simultaneously.
5. Bake at 108°F for 10–12 hours, until thoroughly baked and crispy. Rotate pans after 5–6 hours. Baking time varies depending on what type of oven you use, and the consistency of the batter.

Tip: To make delicious crackers instead, spread a thin, even layer of batter over the entire pan, bake, and divide into pieces.

Almond Crackers with Plum Marmalade
Approximately 15 crackers

These crackers make me think of a British afternoon tea. Enjoy them with homemade plum marmalade and a cup of tea!

scant 1 cup linseeds, plus1 1/3 cup water
1 1/3 cups almond paste, leftover from making Almond Milk, see page 44
3 tbsp. agave nectar or honey

1. Soak linseeds in water for 1/2–4 hours.
2. Mix all ingredients in a bowl until you have a smooth batter.
3. Spread batter into a thin, even layer on parchment-lined cookie sheet.
4. Score the batter lightly with the backside of a knife. It will help break apart the crackers after baking.
5. Bake at 108° F for 8–12 hours. Break apart when ready.

Serve with Plum Marmalade (see page 118).

Crispy Coconut Cookies

Approximately 20 cookies

Are you like me when it comes to eating cookie dough? If that's the case, exchange the water for lemon juice for a more tart taste.

1 1/3 cups cashews
2 cups shredded coconut
3–5 tbsp. honey
3–5 tsp. water or lemon juice

1. Mix cashews in a food processor until they turn into fine cashew flour.
2. Add coconut, and mix until blended with the cashew flour.
3. Add 3 tbsp. of the honey, and mix again. You need to add water or lemon juice to be able to shape batter into cookies. Start by adding 3 tsp., and mix again.
4. Taste for sweetness, and add 2 tbsp. honey if desired. You might also need to add another 2 tsp. of water.
5. Place dough in spoonfuls onto parchment-lined cookie sheet. Use cookie cutters to shape into cookies.
6. Bake at 108°F for 8–12 hours. Rotate the cookie sheets after 4–6 hours.

Oatmeal Cookies with Raisins and Apples

20 cookies

You can buy raw oats in the United States. In Sweden, raw oats are heated during the grain-to-oat process. Sometimes we use them anyway, because they make such delicious cookies. Always choose organic oats!

Tip 1: Keep your hands moist when shaping cookies. It helps prevent the dough from clinging to your fingers.

Tip 2: These cookies are sticky with a shorter baking time. The longer you bake them, the harder they get, and the longer you can store them.

Tip 3: Keep the cookies in the oven overnight. You don't need to set your alarm clock to turn them over—they'll be delicious whenever you wake up!

2 cups oats
scant 2/3 cup dates
scant 1/2 cup raisins
scant 1/2 cup almonds, chopped
2–3 apples, grated

1. Put oats in a food processor and mix until finely ground.
2. Add dates, and mix until blended with the oats.
3. Transfer the batter to a bowl, and stir in raisins and almonds.
4. Add the apples. Feel free to use your hands to mix!
5. Shape batter into cookies and place on parchment-lined cookie sheet. Bake at 108°F for 8–12 hours. Rotate pans after 4–6 hours.

Lisbeth Liljevi, 61 years old, owns a business designing and producing work clothes. She has been living with her partner, Reiner Albrecht, for the last 30 years. During her spare time, Lisbeth enjoys golfing and working out at the gym. She loves berry and mushroom picking in the forest, and she and Reiner take a bicycle trip every summer.

The best thing about raw treats: "You might as well choose healthy snacks if you are a fan of snacking."

Favorites: "It used to be the Apple Pie and the Chocolate Ice Cream, but now the chocolate pastries are my favorites!"

Lillemor Hjärpe, 70 years old, is a retired model and boutique sales associate. This year, Lillemor and her husband Bengt are celebrating their 50th wedding anniversary. They have two grown kids, Maria and Joakim.

Lillemor likes long walks, working out in the gym, and swimming in the ocean in the summertime.

The best part about raw treats: "I'm a dessert person, so it has been fun to try out these treats because they are so much healthier."

Favorite: "Chocolate Pastry."

"You might as well choose healthy snacks if you are a fan of snacking."

Lisbeth Liljevi and Lillemor Hjärpe know each other through a mutual friend. Both women take good care of themselves, and enjoy tasting new dishes or sweets. Their first encounter with raw foods was during a fashion show afterparty, where hors-d'oeuvres and snacks were served, among them a broccoli dish.

Lillemor wanted to know more, and signed up for a raw food workshop. She never imagined she would actually be able to prepare any of the dishes at home; it seemed too complicated.

"I enjoyed most of the dishes we made during the raw food week—but definitely not all of them. I discovered that making raw food dishes is not that complicated, and have since started eating a raw breakfast, consisting of three fruits and cinnamon."

Lisbeth also wanted to learn more about raw foods. She and a friend, Eva, gathered together a group of ten women for a raw food evening. They met at Eva's home and prepared different dishes under guidance.

"I have been dedicated to raw foods ever since, and prepare a lot of vegetable dishes. For breakfast I usually mix together a cream out of fruit and berries. Sometimes I add sunflower seeds to make it more filling, other times I add Turkish yogurt. You can compromise a little bit!"

Lillemor considers the nutrient boost a big plus, along with the fact that raw treats are made without any added sugar.

"My friend, Lotta, and I have made these raw treats for guests, and they were much appreciated! At home I often make apple pie. Even my husband has been curious to try it. Since we've gotten older, we don't like super sugary sweets."

Lisbeth appreciates sweet and delicious treats without any sugar, too, but for entirely different reasons: "I consume way too much sugar as it is. I'm a true 'sugarholic,' and add three spoons of sugar to my coffee. I'd rather quench my thirst with homemade juice than with water."

Despite Lisbeth's love for sugar, she used to prefer to complement a meal with a good appetizer rather than dessert.

"Raw food desserts are not as heavy as regular sweets, and taste much better after a meal."

Her live-in partner agrees, and likes to try the new treats.

"This summer when we had some good friends over, I served Chocolate Ice Cream, Apple Pie, and Peach Pie."

Lisbeth seldom likes to eat an entire apple or banana, so she considers a raw food treat to be a delightful and positive experience.

"It is a delicious way for me to consume fruit and berries!"

Classics
—NEW TASTE TWISTS ON CLASSIC GOODIES

Desserts and other treats that are reminiscent of traditional desserts, but made with a raw twist—by adding nuts, dried fruit, honey, fresh fruit, and berries!

Hazelnut Nougat

Approximately 10 pieces

Henrik and Jessica are "raw foodists" that love nougat. They inspired me to create this Hazelnut Nougat.

scant 1 cup hazelnuts
4 tsp. water
2 tbsp. agave nectar or honey
2 tsp. carob powder

1. Mix hazelnuts in a food processor until they turn into fine hazelnut flour.
2. Add water, agave nectar or honey, carob powder, and mix again.
3. Shape into an oblong hazelnut nougat piece and store in the fridge.

Tip: Make another layer without adding the carob, and then spread over the carob layer for a double nougat treat.

Pears à la After Eight

4 portions

My coauthor recently rediscovered her passion for cacao, and loves my variation of Pears à la After Eight. Go for it, Irmela!

4 pears, juicy, soft, and sliced

FILLING/BRAZIL NUT CREAM:
scant 1 cup Brazil nuts
8 drops peppermint oil
1 tbsp. agave nectar or honey

TOPPING:
Chocolate Sauce, see page 120

1. Soak Brazil nuts for 8–24 hours.
2. Mix Brazil nuts in a food processor until finely chopped.
3. Add peppermint oil and agave nectar or honey. Mix again.
4. Spread pear slices over the bottom of an oven dish, or four small ramekins.
5. Spread Brazil nut cream over the pears.
6. Pour Chocolate Sauce on top.
7. Store in the fridge for 1–2 hours before serving.

Stuffed Apples
4 portions

When I grew up in Sweden, we used to eat oven-baked apples in the fall. Red apples with stuffing are delicious—without the baking part!

4 red apples

FILLING:
the pulp from the apples
1 cup almonds
4 tsp. honey
2 tsp. honey

SERVE WITH:
Vanilla Sauce, see page 47

1. Core the apples (an apple corer makes it easier!).
2. Scoop out 2/3 of the inside of the apples.
3. Chop almonds finely in food processor.
4. Add apple pulp, honey, and cinnamon. Mix again.
5. Place apples on a serving plate, and stuff filling inside each apple.
6. Serve with Vanilla Sauce.

Tip: Vary the recipe by substituting other nuts for the almonds. Hazelnuts are a delicious choice for the filling.

Layer Cake

4 portions

My seven-year-old niece Vera wanted to spread this cake on top of her sandwich. Instead, she ended up eating the entire cake straight out of the dish!

LAYER 1/ALMOND BATTER:
2 1/2 cups almonds
3 tbsp. Almond Milk or water
6 tbsp. agave nectar

LAYER 2/PINE NUT & CAROB CREAM:
2 1/2 cups pine nuts
1 cup water
3 tbsp. coconut oil
3 tbsp. carob powder
3 tbsp. agave nectar or honey

1. Chop almonds finely in a food processor.
2. Add Almond Milk or water, and agave nectar. Mix again.
3. Press half of layer 1 in the bottom of a dish.
4. Mix pine nuts and water in a mixer.
5. Add agave nectar or honey, coconut oil, and carob powder. Mix again.
6. Spread half of the pine nut & carob cream over the first layer.
7. Spread the rest of the almond batter on top of the second layer.
8. Top with a layer of pine nut & carob cream.
9. Put in the fridge for 1–2 hours before serving.

Citron Fromage with Strawberry Sauce

2 portions

Make your own Citron Fromage from scratch. Sour meets strawberry-sweet in this delightful treat.

CITRON FROMAGE:

scant 1 cup cashews
scant 1 cup fresh lemon juice
1 tbsp. water
1 tbsp. coconut oil
1 tbsp. agave nectar

STRAWBERRY SAUCE:

8 ounces defrosted strawberries, or scant 2 cups fresh strawberries
6 apricots
scant 1/4 cup soak water from the apricots (only if you are using fresh strawberries)

1. Soak apricots 4–10 hours.
2. Mix cashews in a food processor until they turn into cashew flour.
3. Add lemon juice and water.
4. Melt coconut oil in a water bath.
5. Add coconut oil and agave nectar to cashew mixture.
6. Put in the fridge for an hour.
7. Mix ingredients for the Strawberry Sauce.
8. Drizzle Strawberry Sauce over the Citron Fromage just before serving.

Passion Dream

2 portions

Like a golden dream—beautiful and delicious!

1 1/3 cups cashews
scant 1/2 cup water
1 tbsp. honey
1 tbsp. coconut oil
3 passion fruits

1. Mix cashews in a food processor until they turn into cashew flour.
2. Add water, honey, and coconut oil. Mix until blended.
3. Scoop out seeds from two of the passion fruits. Add to the blend, and mix.
4. Transfer to two dishes or one bowl. Put in the fridge approximately 2 hours prior to serving.
5. Garnish with half a passion fruit per portion.

Drinks
—FROM FRESH AND FRUITY TO CHOCOLATY DIVINE!

Luxuriously delicious drinks, made out of real produce. I love making smoothies because I am a little bit lazy! Just use what's already in your fridge, throw it all in the blender, mix for a few minutes, and it's done! Try out different ideas and variations until you find your own favorite. Drink the smoothie right away—it's best when fresh—but you can keep it in the fridge in a tightly sealed jar for up to 24 hours.

Nectarine & Strawberry Smoothie
2 glasses

A refreshing, drinkable dessert that will cool you off on a warm summer evening. Add lime, and the smoothie will remind you of a frozen margarita!

2 cups fresh orange juice, or 2 cups water
2 nectarines, cut into pieces
25 strawberries, fresh or frozen
2 tbsp. honey
juice of 1 lime
ice cubes, optional

1. Pour orange juice or water into a blender.
2. Add nectarine pieces, and mix.
3. Add strawberries. If you are using frozen strawberries, add them while the blender is running.
4. Add honey and lime juice, mix, and you'll have a refreshing smoothie!
5. If you want a colder smoothie, add some ice cubes and mix again.

Raw Chocolate Milk

2 glasses

I used to drink a lot of chocolate milk when I was a little girl. This variation makes my body and mind much more alert!

scant 1 cup Cashew Cream with Pear, see page 121
1 1/3 cup water
2 tbsp. raw cacao
3 tsp. honey or agave nectar
ice cubes, optional

1. Put Cashew Cream in a blender and add water. Mix.
2. Add cacao and honey. Mix again.
3. Serve in tall glasses. Add ice cubes if you want the drink chilled.

Chocolate Mint Drink

2 glasses

A delicious and refreshing drink with cacao and peppermint.
Great if you're feeling a little bit slouchy in the afternoon!

2 cups Almond Milk, see page 44
5 dates
4 drops peppermint oil
1–2 tbsp. cacao powder
ice cubes, optional

1. Put all ingredients except for the ice in a blender, and mix.
2. Pour the chocolate drink into beautiful glasses.
3. Serve with ice for an even more refreshing taste!

Hempseed Smoothie with Nectarine

2 glasses

Vary your Hempseed Smoothie with different fruits and berries.

scant 1 cup shelled hempseeds
2 cups water
2 nectarines, cut into pieces
4 dates
1 tsp. cinnamon powder

1. Mix hempseeds with water.
2. Add nectarines, dates, and cinnamon. Mix again.

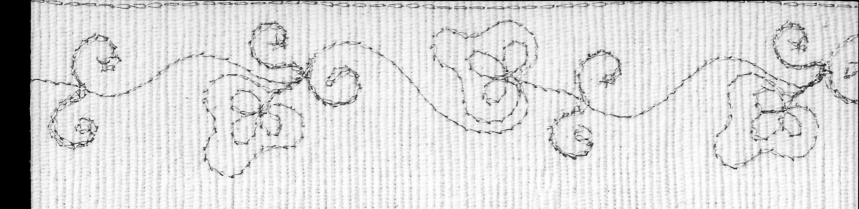

Chai Hempseed Smoothie
2 glasses

The hempseeds add a satisfying quality to this smoothie, and your body receives high quality protein and healthy fats.

scant 1 cup shelled hempseeds
2 cups water
5 dates
1 tbsp. honey
1 tsp. cinnamon powder
1/2 tsp. nutmeg, grated or powdered
1/2 tsp. cloves

1. Mix hempseeds and water in a blender.
2. Add dates, honey, and spices. Mix again.

Goji & Blueberry Smoothie

2 glasses

An antioxidant boost! Drink for breakfast, as a dessert, or as a healthy snack.

scant 1/2 cup goji berries
scant 1 cup blueberries, fresh or defrosted
2 cups Almond Milk, see page 44
5 dates
water, optional

1. Soak goji berries 1/2–3 hours.
2. Drain the goji berries from the soak water. Mix all the ingredients.
3. Add water until you achieve desired consistency.

Brazil Nut Dream with Vanilla

2 glasses

The simplest things in life are usually the best. You can truly distinguish the vanilla in this smooth Brazil nut milk. You can keep it in the fridge for up to three days.

2 cups Brazil nut milk
1 tsp. organic vanilla powder
4 dates

1. Make Brazil nut milk the same way you would make Almond Milk (see page 44).
2. Mix all the ingredients together.

Thirst Quenching Delights for Hot Summer Days!

Citron Lemonade
One pitcher

1 1/3 cups fresh lemon juice
3 tbsp. honey
2 1/2 cups water
crushed ice, optional

1. Mix lemon juice with water and honey.
2. Pour into a pitcher.
3. If you want ice, crush it in a blender and add to lemonade.

Red Ice Tea
One pitcher

34 ounces red tea, like rooibos
2 tbsp. honey, optional
1 lemon, cut into thin slices
1/2 lemon balm herb pot

1. Let the tea rest in cold water overnight, or brew and let it cool off.
2. Sweeten with honey if you want, and mix.
3. Pour the tea into a pitcher and drop in the lemon slices and lemon balm.

Strawberry Lemonade
One pitcher

scant 1 cup fresh lemon juice
34 ounces strawberries, fresh or frozen
2 tbsp. honey
2 1/2 cups carbonated water or regular water
ice

1. Mix lemon juice, strawberries, and honey in a blender.
2. If you are using regular water, add and mix again.
   If you are using carbonated water, add, and stir with
   a spoon.
3. Pour into a pitcher and add ice and/or frozen
   strawberries.

Side Dishes & Other Small Snacks

Jazz up the delicious delights a bit, with sauces, marmalades, creams, and other small and tasty snacks to add to your raw treats and desserts. Try the Chocolate Dipped Pecans, or the Marinated Nectarines. They're tasty on their own, and absolutely yummy with any of the ice creams.

Chocolate Covered Pecans

Nuts with a little extra something! You can also try this recipe with different nuts.

scant 1/2 cup pecans
2 tbsp. Chocolate Sauce, see page 120

1. Dip pecans in Chocolate Sauce.
2. Place chocolate covered nuts on a plate and put in the fridge until ready to serve.

Plum Marmalade

Delicious on raw food crackers. Top off with Cashew Cream for added luxury.

4 plums
4 apricots
1 tbsp. soak water

1. Soak apricots for 4–10 hours.
2. Mix ingredients in a blender until you have a smooth blend.
3. Store in a tightly sealed jar in the fridge.

Date Marmalade

Date marmalade is excellent to keep in the fridge, ready to spread on crackers, or to add to desserts and treats, or the morning fruit salad!

1 1/3 cup dates
scant 1/2 cup water

1. Put pitted dates in a bowl.
2. If using dried dates, soak them for a few hours; just add enough water to cover them. If using fresh dates, you don't need to soak them.
3. Run the blender or food processor.
4. The marmalade will last about a week in a tightly sealed container in the fridge.

Chocolate Sauce

Use this Chocolate Sauce to garnish your pies and pastries, or drizzle over ice cream and fruit salad.

scant 1 cup coconut oil
scant 2/3 cup cacao powder
scant 1/4 cup agave nectar
scant 1/2 cup walnuts or pecans, roughly chopped, or scant 1/2 cup cacao pieces, optional

1. Melt coconut oil in a water bath.
2. Stir with other ingredients in a bowl.
3. If you want a chunky Chocolate Sauce, stir in some nuts or cacao pieces.

Chocolate Belts

One Tray

Sometimes I get crazy cravings for something chocolaty and chewy. Those times are perfect for a load of chocolate belts!

3 bananas
3 tbsp. cacao powder
1 tsp. vanilla powder

1. Mix all ingredients in a food processor.
2. Spread a thin layer over a parchment-lined cookie sheet.
3. Dehydrate in the oven at 108°F for about 8 hours. It's ready when it's leathery like toffee, and you can cut it into strips, or belts.

Tip: You can also make these out of banana chocolate ice cream batter.

Cashew Cream

Organic vanilla powder, with its full vanilla aroma, complements this Cashew Cream, but you can skip the vanilla if you want a more neutral cream.

scant 1 cup cashews
scant 1 cup water
1/2 vanilla pod or 1 tsp. organic vanilla powder
1 pear, cut into pieces
1 tbsp. honey or agave nectar, or 4 dates

1. Mix cashews in a food processor until you have fine cashew flour.
2. Dilute with water, and mix again.
3. Add vanilla pod or vanilla powder, pear, and honey or agave nectar or dates.
4. Taste, and determine if you need to add more vanilla or water.

Alternative: Follow the recipe without adding the pear and the honey or agave nectar or dates.

Sesame Cream

Cream that is loaded with calcium from the tiny, nutritious sesame seeds! Delicious with any of the velvety creams!

scant 1 cup sesame seeds, unpeeled
scant 2 cups water or soak water from the dried fruit
5 dried figs, apricots, or dates

1. Soak the dried fruit for 4–10 hours.
2. Mix sesame seeds with water.
3. Add soaked fruit, mix again.

Tip: You can also sweeten the cream with bananas, honey, or agave nectar.

Marinated Nectarines

Enjoy fresh herbs with your desserts.

2 nectarines, cut into squares

MARINADE:
1 tbsp. honey
1/2 an herb pot of lemon balm or mint (a handful), roughly chopped
1 tbsp. fresh lemon juice

TOPPING:
2 tbsp. almonds, chopped

1. Mix all the ingredients for the marinade.
2. Soak nectarines in the marinade for about an hour.
3. Garnish with chopped almonds before serving.

Tip: This treat is delicious with the Banana Ice Cream.

Inspiration

BOOKS:
RAWvolution, Matt Amsden, William Morrow, 2006.
Healthful Cuisine, Anna Maria Clement, and others, Healthful Communications, Inc., 2007.
RAW: The UNcook Book, Juliano, with Erica Lenkert, Regan Books, 1999.
Raw Food/Real World, Matthew Kenney, Sarma Melngailis, William Morrow Cookbooks, 2005.
The Sunfood Diet Success System, David Wolfe, North Atlantic Books, 2008.

WEBSITES:
www.thegardendiet.com
www.rawspirit.org
www.renegadehealth.com

Contact the Authors:

Erica Palmcrantz Aziz, raw food enthusiast
www.rawfoodbyerica.se

Irmela Lilja, health and personal development journalist
contact via publishing company

A Warm Thank You!

To our families and friends who gave us support during our work on the manuscript,
and who continue to do the same on life's journey.
To our enthusiastic editor, Monica Katarina Frisk.
To the super nice Ronny Karlgren at Pathos Reklambyrå in Orsa.
To the photographer, Anna Hult, for her energy, beautiful pictures, and playful ideas.

Recipe Index

My Own Notes